SUMMARY
of
FEELING GOOD

The New Mood Therapy

by David D. Burns, M.D.

A FastReads Book Summary with
Key Takeaways & Analysis

TABLE OF CONTENTS

EXECUTIVE SUMMARY

The book *Feeling Good: The New Mood Therapy* written by David D. Burns talks about cognitive therapy as a treatment for depression and other emotional disorders.

The book is divided into seven sections. The first section of the book introduces us to the basic concept of cognitive therapy and the reason behind its popularity. He reveals the various twisted thinking patterns that lead us to depression. The second and third sections of the book reveal some useful self-help techniques that can help us treat our depression. The fourth section of the book sheds some light on what it really means to recover from depression. It explains the difference between *feeling better* and *getting better* and shows how to acquire self-esteem and self-confidence. The fifth section focuses on suicidal urges, their root cause, and how to assess them. The sixth section shows us how cognitive therapy techniques can help us cope with the stresses of our daily lives. In this part, the author gives a behind-the-scenes picture of his job as a therapist and shows how the techniques he preaches have helped him cope with the strains of everyday living. The seventh section answers the question of whether our depression and mood problems have anything to do with our body chemistry or environment. The author debunks some of the most common myths held by depressed individuals regarding psychotherapy and antidepressant drug medication. He also discusses some general facts regarding drug medication and provides a brief overview of some widely prescribed antidepressants.

This book is a great resource not only for depressed individuals but also for people from all walks of life. It can be quite helpful for people looking to experience personal growth and enhance their self-esteem.

INTRODUCTION

In the last three decades, interest in cognitive therapy has risen mainly because of the following three reasons:

• The basic concept behind cognitive therapy is very straightforward and simple.

• Not only is cognitive therapy helpful in coping with depression and anxiety, it is as helpful as anti-depressants.

• Many self-help books have created awareness and demand for cognitive therapy.

But what is cognitive therapy really?

Cognition means thought. It's what you are thinking about at any time. These thoughts affect how we feel. In short, thoughts create feelings. The principle that governs cognitive therapy is that our feelings have more to do with our thoughts than what happens in our life.

Shakespeare wrote: *"For there is nothing either good or bad, but thinking makes it so."*

When a person feels depressed, he thinks it has something to do with the bad things that have happened to him. A person may think he is inferior because he got rejected by someone he loved or because he is convinced that he is not smart and attractive enough. Of course, there is an element of truth there because bad things do happen to us. But the theory that our negative feelings are the result of these life experiences can make us victims for our entire lives. We become victims when we think that the causes of our bad moods are beyond our control. We cannot do much to change other people or how they treat us but we certainly can do something to change the way we think. Changing the way we think can have a positive influence on our mood. This is what cognitive therapy is about.

Key Takeaways:

• Cognitive therapy is as helpful as anti-depressants in coping with depression and anxiety.

• Cognitive therapy is based on the principle that our thoughts create our feelings.

• Changing the way we think can have a powerful impact on our mood.

PART 1: THEORY & RESEARCH

1. A Breakthrough in the Treatment of Mood Disorders

Depression, the number one health problem across the globe, has caused a spike in suicide rates. The death rate due to depression is climbing up despite the large number of antidepressants produced by the health industry. The good news is that you can overcome depression by using some simple mood-control techniques. Research studies have shown that this new approach to treating emotional disorders helps overcome symptoms of depression faster than the conventional methods or even drugs.

Cognitive therapy is a technology of mood modification that can be applied on one's own. It helps an individual experience personal growth and overcome depression effectively. These mood modification techniques provide:

• Relief from symptoms of milder depression in as early as twelve weeks.

• Clear understanding of why people get moody and what they can do to elevate their mood.

• Practical and effective strategies to get your mood under control.

• Prevention from future mood swings and promotion of personal growth.

There are three principles that cognitive therapy is based upon:

1. All our moods are the result of our thoughts or cognitions. Cognition is how we look at and interpret things. It includes the messages we give ourselves about someone or something.

2. When we feel depressed, we think negatively and everything around us looks dark and gloomy. We even start believing that things will always stay negative.

3. Our negative thoughts contain gross distortions. In other words, our twisted thinking is the cause of our emotional turmoil.

In short, our depression is the result of mental distortions.

Key Takeaways:

• Cognitive therapy helps overcome symptoms of depression faster than the conventional psychotherapy.

• It provides understanding of why we get moody, offers effective self-control strategies, and prevents future mood swings.

• Depression and other emotional disorders are the result of our twisted thinking.

2. How to Diagnose Your Moods: The First Step in the Cure

Regardless of how severe your emotional disorder is, the first step to getting better is making the decision to help yourself. Normal depression is not a cause of concern because we all have problems in our daily life. Applying cognitive therapy techniques, however, can make a big difference in our thinking.

Mild depression can be treated through self-help efforts, but prolonged mild depression does require professional treatment. This type of mild chronic depression is called **dysthymic disorder**. People who suffer from *dysthymic disorder* are negative and gloomy for the greater part of their life. Moderate depression should be taken seriously because it indicates intense suffering. Prolonged moderate depression should be a cause for alarm. Extreme or severe depression indicates a level of suffering that is unbearable. It can be dangerous because it may trigger suicidal impulses. An individual should not attempt to treat this type of depression on his or her own. However, applying self-help techniques while receiving psychotherapy or drug medication can speed up recovery.

Key Takeaways:

• The first step to getting better is making the decision to help yourself.

• The use of self-help techniques while receiving psychotherapy or drug medication can speed up recovery from depression.

3. Understanding Your Moods: You Feel the Way You Think

Our bad feelings are the product of our distorted negative thinking. Our negative thinking and pessimistic attitude are the reasons why depression symptoms develop and persist. The author writes, *"Intense negative thinking always brings a depressive episode."*

When you feel depressed, identify the negative thought that had flooded your mind just before or during the depressive episode. These thoughts are the real cause of your bad mood and by modifying them you can elevate your mood. When intense negative thinking becomes a part of our lives negative thoughts become our **automatic thoughts**. They become so natural to us that they flow through our minds automatically all the time.

Our emotions are the result of the way we perceive things. The relationship between our thoughts and feelings can be understood in this way:

• When we look at things or events, we interpret them and give them meaning.

• When interpreting these events, a chain of thoughts runs through our minds and an **internal dialogue** takes place.

• Our thoughts create our feelings. Our brain processes the events and gives them meaning before we actually experience an emotional reaction.

In other words, it's not what happens to us that changes our mood; it's our perceptions that cause this change. We feel depressed because our thoughts are distorted and illogical. Here are ten cognitive distortions that cause depression:

1. All or nothing thinking: evaluating things in black-or-white. For example, considering yourself a failure on getting a B grade instead of an A.

2. Overgeneralization: believing that the one unpleasant event that happened will occur again and again. For example, thinking you will never get a date just because one girl turned you down.

3. Mental filter: focusing on the one negative detail of an event so much that the entire event looks dark and negative. For example, missing a few questions in an exam and dwelling on them so hard that you conclude you will not pass the exam.

4. Disqualifying the positive: rejecting positive experiences. For example, thinking *"they are just being nice"* when people compliment you.

5. Jumping to conclusions: making a negative interpretation even when there are no concrete facts to support it. For example, thinking your friend is ignoring you when in fact he was so absorbed in his thoughts that he didn't notice you (mind reading) or thinking you will be depressed forever and causing this prediction to make you feel hopeless (fortune teller error).

6. Magnification and minimization: exaggerating someone else's achievement or qualities while shrinking your own or magnifying the importance of your mistakes and faults while minimizing someone else's. For example, *"I made a mistake, my reputation is ruined."*

7. Emotional reasoning: assuming things are negative just because they feel negative to you. For example, telling yourself, *"I feel like a failure, therefore I must be a failure."*

8. Should statements: putting yourself under pressure by saying you *should* or *must* do this. Or directing *should* statements at others. For example, thinking *"he ought to be punctual"* when someone is late.

9. Labeling and mislabeling: forming negative self-image of yourself or others (labeling) or describing a situation inaccurately (mislabeling). For example, losing a match and saying, *"I am a born loser"* (labeling) or eating an ice cream while being on diet and saying, *"I'm a pig"* (mislabeling).

10. Personalization: feeling responsible for a negative event which in fact wasn't in your control. For example, thinking *"I must be a bad mother"* when your kid gets a poor grade.

Key Takeaways:

• It's our perceptions that change our mood, not what actually happens to us.

• Negative thoughts grow so obvious that they become our automatic thoughts.

• We feel depressed because our thoughts are distorted and illogical.

PART II: PRACTICAL APPLICATIONS

4. Start by Building Self-Esteem

Depressed individuals have low self-esteem and a poor self-image. According to Dr. Aaron Beck, the self-image of a depressed person is characterized by 4 D's: feeling **Defeated**, **Defective**, **Deserted**, and **Deprived**. The question is how accurate your feelings of inadequacy are. Is it important to look at what you think about yourself? Your self-worth, what you think about yourself, plays a huge role in how you feel. Everything we say about ourselves when we insist we are worthless is usually based on arguments that make no sense at all. Our self-esteem and self-love are far more important than how much we are loved by other people or what we accomplish.

A study by Drs. Aaron Beck and David Braff indicated that depressed people begin to lose their capacity to think clearly. Therefore, the more depressed a person is, the more twisted his thinking is. The mental distortions discussed in the previous chapter are the reasons behind our sense of worthlessness. The most common distortion behind our feeling of worthlessness is the *all-or-nothing* thinking.

There are, however, some techniques which can be used to boost your self-esteem:

• **Talk back to your internal critic:** The self-degrading statements we tell ourselves, such as "I'm no good, I'm a loser," are the reason behind our low self-esteem. Every time you have a self-critical thought, write it down and try to identify why your thoughts are distorted. Then come up with a rational response to counter the automatic negative thought.

• **Mental biofeedback:** Monitor the number of negative thoughts that cross your mind with the help of a wrist counter and record it in a log daily.

• **Cope, don't mope:** But how can you force yourself to think differently when your problems are realistic? Labeling yourself as inadequate and worthless clouds the real problems in your life. Once you are able to counter the self-criticism and negative labels, you can counter the real problems in your life.

Key Takeaways:

• Depressed people have low self-esteem and a poor self-image.

• What we think about ourselves plays a huge role in how we feel.

• Our self-esteem and self-love are more important than how much we are loved by other people or what we accomplish.

5. Do-Nothingism: How to Beat It

Changing the way you think helps elevate your mood, but getting up and actually doing something is a more effective approach. The only problem is that a depressed individual does not feel the urge to do anything. The acts of do-nothingness and procrastination are major obstacles in treating your emotional disorder. The most popular explanations for this behavior include:

• You think you're too lazy

• You have a drive to be self-destructive

• You are passive-aggressive

• You must be getting a reward (e.g. getting attention) from your do-nothingness

Mindsets that are commonly linked with do-nothingness and procrastination include:

Hopelessness: You forget that you ever felt positive in the past or will do so in the future.

Helplessness: You think that your moods are affected by things beyond your control.

Overwhelming yourself: You overwhelm yourself by unnecessarily magnifying a task, think that you must do everything at once, or worry about other things instead of focusing on the task at hand.

Jumping to conclusions: You think you *can't* do anything that will make you feel better without even trying to do so.

Self-labeling: When you label yourself as a "procrastinator," you automatically do not expect much from yourself.

Undervaluing the rewards: You fail to take action because you think the reward will not be worth the effort.

Perfectionism: You set inappropriate or unrealistic goals and want to be a perfectionist in everything you do.

Fear of failure: You refuse to try something because you think you will fail.

Fear of success: You fear success because you think others will expect more from you or that you will fail to keep up and eventually everyone will know you are a loser.

Fear of disapproval or criticism: You are afraid of trying something new or making a mistake because you think others will criticize or reject you.

Coercion and resentment: You put yourself under pressure with unnecessary *should* statements and then eventually feel burdened and resentful.

Low frustration tolerance: You expect that you will be able to solve your problems easily or rapidly. When obstacles come in the way or things get tough, you panic or retaliate.

Guilt and self-blame: You think you have disappointed others and do not feel like doing anything.

Key Takeaways:

• Depressed individuals do not feel the urge to do anything.

• The acts of do-nothingness and procrastination are major obstacles in treating your emotional disorder.

6. Verbal Judo: Learn to Talk Back When You're Under the Fire of Criticism

Self-criticism may not only come from your internal conversation; it may also be triggered by others' remarks. When someone criticizes you, negative thoughts automatically begin to flow through your mind. These thoughts are what trigger a negative emotional reaction, not the other person's remarks. Keep in mind that there's only one person who can put you down, and that's *you*!

This technique can help you handle verbal abuse without losing your self-esteem.

Step 1—Empathy: When someone criticizes you, ask them questions to find out exactly what they mean. Do not be judgmental or defensive.

Step 2—Disarming the critic: Find a way to agree with your critic whether they are right or wrong. If you find it difficult to agree with them, find some part of truth in what they say.

Step 3—Feedback and negotiation: Now explain your position tactfully to negotiate the differences.

Key Takeaways:

• Self-criticism may come from our internal conversation and may be triggered by other people's remarks.

• No one has the power to put you down except you!

7. Feeling Angry? What's Your IQ?

There are two primary methods to deal with anger:

Anger turned inward: You turn your aggression inward and try to absorb it. This is not a healthy solution as it corrodes you from the inside.

Anger turned outward: You express your anger and try to ventilate your feelings. Although this solution is considered healthy since it helps you feel better, it has its downside. Not only will people dislike you, this approach does not teach you how to deal with others without getting angry.

Fortunately, there is a third solution: stop creating your anger. If anger does not exist, then you won't have to make the choice of turning it inward or ventilating it. Exactly how can you decide whether feeling angry is in your best interests or not? Ask yourself two questions:

• Are you angry at someone who has intentionally hurt you?

• Will being angry help you achieve your desired goals?

The following methods will help you reduce your anger when it is not productive:

Develop the desire: List down the advantages and disadvantages of feeling and expressing anger, compare them and decide whether your anger is productive.

Cool those hot thoughts: List down all the negative thoughts flowing through your mind and substitute them with objective and cool thoughts.

Imagining techniques: Conjure up a funny image of the person you are angry at in your mind. Or think about other things, read a book, go jogging, etc.

Rewrite the rules: Crafting unrealistic rules about relationships (e.g. *"I should be treated courteously"* or *"if I am nice to people, they should be nice to me"*) can cause us to be upset when other people fail to meet our expectations. The solution is to replace your *should* and *shouldn't* rules with more realistic ones. For example, *"All people are different, some will be nice to me and some won't be."*

Learn to expect craziness: Changing your expectations of people will help reduce frustration when they fail to meet those expectations.

Enlightened manipulation: Focus on the positive things that people do instead of the negatives. Reward the desired behavior in them instead of punishing them for the undesired behavior.

"Should" reduction: List down all the reasons that support your 'should' statements and replace them with more realistic ones that actually make sense.

Negotiating strategies: Try negotiating instead of expressing anger.

Accurate empathy: Understanding other people's thoughts and motivations accurately will help you find out why they act the way they do even though you do not like their actions.

Putting it all together: Cognitive rehearsal: List down the situations that make you angry and which you would like to learn to handle. Rate them from 1 (least upsetting) to 10 (most upsetting). Fantasize the least upsetting situation in your mind and imagine how you would handle it effectively using the techniques you have learned. Practice handling the situation in your imagination. This rehearsal will help you cope with the situation when it actually happens to you. Work your way from the least upsetting to the most infuriating situations.

Key Takeaways

• The best way to deal with anger is to stop creating it.

• Always ask yourself, is feeling angry in your best interest?

8. Ways of Defeating Guilt

You experience guilt when you have the following thoughts in mind:

• You have done something you shouldn't have or vice versa

• Your bad behavior shows that you are a bad person

Are your guilty feelings healthy or self-defeating? Use the following criteria to find out:

• Did you intentionally do the thing you shouldn't have done? Are you expecting yourself to be a perfectionist?

• Are you labeling yourself as a bad person because of this action? Do your thoughts contain cognitive distortions such as *overgeneralizing* or *magnifying*?

• Is your regret realistic? Does it result from the awareness of your action and its negative impact? Is the intensity and duration of the guilt appropriate to the situation?

• Are you learning from your mistakes and developing a plan for change? Or are you punishing yourself in a nonproductive and destructive manner?

Some ways of getting rid of inappropriate guilt and increasing your self-respect include:

Daily record of dysfunctional thoughts: Record the situations that lead to your guilty feelings, identify the cognitive distortions in your thoughts, and come up with rational and objective responses to counter your guilt.

'Should' removal techniques: Get rid of *should* statements by analyzing their advantages and disadvantages. Understand that your *should* statements are not realistic. Replace your *should* statements with more rational ones.

Learn to stick to your guns: Understand that people can use your guilt to manipulate you. This will be destructive not only to yourself, but to others.

Anti-whiner technique: When a whiner, especially a loved one, complains about something and you try to offer a suggestion, they take your suggestion as criticism and complain more. Instead, find a way to agree with them and say something genuinely complimentary in order to help them calm down.

Moorey Moaner Method: This is another technique to deal with a person who moans about their personal problems. Find a way to agree with them and then divert their attention to something positive in the complaint.

Developing perspective: You feel guilty when you feel responsible for other people's actions, feelings, or for naturally occurring events. Identify the cognitive distortion in your thoughts and develop a rational response to your automatic guilty thoughts.

Key Takeaways:

• We experience guilt when we think we have done something we shouldn't have (and vice versa) or that we are a bad person because of our bad behavior.

• It is always better to analyze whether our guilty feelings are healthy or self-defeating.

PART III: "REALISTIC" DEPRESSIONS

9. Sadness Is Not Depression

There's a myth that our "realistic problems" (poverty, illness, bankruptcy etc.) lead to "realistic depression." In fact, there's no such thing as a "realistic depression." So, how do we differentiate between healthy and unhealthy negative feelings? In simple words, what is the difference between sadness and depression?

• Sadness is a normal emotion whereas depression is an illness.

• Sadness comes without distortion and does not involve loss of self-esteem. It results from a realistic perception of a negative event in an undistorted way. Depression always comes from distorted thinking and involves loss of self-esteem.

• Sadness has a time limit whereas depression has none.

When a negative event takes place, your emotions result from the thoughts and the meanings you attach to the event. A major portion of your suffering is due to the cognitive distortions in your thoughts. When you remove the distortions, coping with the real issue becomes easier and less painful.

Key Takeaways:

• Our realistic problems do not lead to realistic depression.

• Sadness is a normal healthy emotion without distortion, whereas depression is an illness that always results from distorted thinking.

some people don't like me in
AA, they don't like my shoes

↓

what does it mean

↓

People think I'm being fake

↓

what does it mean

↓

I'm not being fake, ~~and just~~
ive lived a fake life for so long
I constantly question myself and

PART IV: PREVENTION AND PERSONAL GROWTH

if what I'm saying is true. So
I ~~feel~~ make this assumption that
people don't like me with no
evidence to support it. Not everyone
is going to like me. But the real
question is "do I like me?"
Today the answer is yes.

10. The Cause of It All

Patients begin feeling well at the end of the therapy. It is important to note that a residue of their mood disorders usually remains inside them. If this residue is not eliminated, then the patient is at risk of attacks of depression in future. It turns out, there's a difference between **feeling better** and **getting better**. *Feeling better* simply means that the depression symptoms have disappeared temporarily. *Getting better* means:

• Knowing why you got depressed in the first place

• Understanding how and why you got better

• Gaining self-esteem and self-confidence

• Finding the causes of your depression

Even when your negative thoughts have reduced as a result of therapy, some **silent assumptions** remain lurking in your mind. These *silent assumptions* define our personal worth and tell us why we become depressed. For example:

• *I must perform perfectly or I will fail*

• *If someone criticizes me, it means there is something wrong with me*

In short, these *silent assumptions* represent your Achilles' heel.

One way to identify a *silent assumption* is the **vertical-arrow technique**. The method involves the following steps:

• Write down your automatic thought

• Draw a downward arrow just beneath your thought and ask yourself, "*Suppose your automatic thought was true, why would it be disturbing you? What does it mean to you?*"

• Write down the next automatic thought that comes to your mind

• Again, draw a downward arrow just beneath your second thought and ask yourself the same question

• Repeat the process. The chain of thoughts will expose your *silent assumption* which is causing you to feel depressed.

For example:

Automatic Thought #1: *My boyfriend promised to call me but he didn't.*

• *What does it mean to me?*

Automatic Thought #2: *This means that he is ignoring me.*

• *If that were true, what would it mean to me?*

Automatic Thought #3: *It would mean that there's something wrong with me.*

• *If that were true, what would it mean to me?*

Automatic Thought #4: *It would mean that I will be rejected.*

• *If that happens, what would it mean to me?*

Automatic Thought #5: *It would mean that I will always get rejected.*

• *If that happens, what would it mean to me?*

Automatic Thought #6: *It would mean that I will be lonely and miserable.*

This method reveals the underlying *silent assumption* that "*If I'm not loved, it means that I'm worthless.*" Or, "*I will always be alone and miserable.*"

Key Takeaways:

• *Silent assumptions* are the statements of our personal worth that explain why we get depressed.

• If not properly eliminated, silent assumptions can put us at risk of depression attacks in the future.

• *Feeling better* means that the depression symptoms have disappeared temporarily. Whereas *getting better* means knowing why and how you got depressed, understanding how you recovered, finding the root cause of your depression, and gaining self-esteem.

11. The Approval Addiction

It feels awful when people disapprove of you. Let's look at the following silent assumption:

"If someone disapproves of me, it means everyone will disapprove of me. This means that there is something wrong with me."

Exactly why do we fear disapproval? And why are we addicted to approval?

Of course, you feel good when you get positive feedback. However, you must keep in mind that it's your thoughts and feelings that elevate your mood—and not what others say—unless you believe their compliment to be true and valid. Hence, it's your belief that makes you feel good. The more you become addicted to approval, the more vulnerable you become to other people's opinion of you.

In order to free yourself from fear of disapproval and approval addiction, take the following steps:

Cost-benefit analysis: Compare the advantages and disadvantages of believing that disapproval makes you feel worthless. Once you have done this, you will be able to judge whether approval addiction is healthy for you.

Rewrite the assumption: Write a *silent assumption* that's more realistic. For example, *"Disapproval may make me feel uncomfortable but it doesn't mean I'm worthless. Approval may make me feel good but I don't need someone else's approval in order to be a worthwhile person."*

The self-respect blueprint: Write a short essay on why it is irrational to fear disapproval. List down the reasons why disapproval is uncomfortable but not fatal.

Verbal techniques: In addition to thinking differently about disapproval, try to behave differently toward people who disapprove of you. Use the *disarming* technique introduced in Chapter 6.

Rejection is not your fault: Rejection is the worst form of pain someone can inflict on you. Have a look at some common types of rejection:

Adolescent rejection: People turn you down because of your appearance or personality.

Make sure you do not sell yourself short by thinking you are inferior. Boost your self-esteem, give genuine compliments to people instead of waiting for them to accept or reject you. Express interest in them and talk about what excites them.

Angry rejection: People turn you down because of your behavior.

Consider modifying your behavior if it bothers a lot of people. However, keep in mind that we all have imperfections.

Manipulative rejection: People manipulate you by threatening to turn you down.

This indicates that the person manipulating you has poor interpersonal skills and low tolerance for frustration.

Recovering from disapproval or rejection: Keep in mind that life goes on and that it's your thoughts doing the emotional damage and not the rejection. The **grieving method** can help you cope with long-term grief following the death or loss of a loved one. Schedule a period of 5-10 minutes in your everyday routine and allow yourself to grieve, cry, and moan lonely in pain. This technique speeds up the grieving process and helps you recover faster.

Key Takeaways:

• It's not the compliment that makes you feel good; it's your belief that the compliment is true that makes you feel so.

• The more you become addicted to approval, the more vulnerable you become to other people's opinion of you.

• Rejection is the worst form of pain that can be inflicted on you.

12. The Love Addiction

The second silent assumption pertains to love addiction:

"I cannot be happy unless I am truly loved."

This need or demand for love in order to be happy is called **dependency**. It means that you are incapable of taking charge of your emotional life.

Is love a need or a demand? When you take love as a need, it shows that you need someone else to be worthwhile. Getting independence from this need does not mean that you will end up alone.

• Being independent does not mean you have to be alone, it means that you can be happy even when you are alone. Being lonely and dependent, on the other hand, forces you farther into isolation because you feel deprived of love.

• Being independent means that your feelings are secure and other people cannot regulate your moods.

• Being independent is about loving yourself and having high self-esteem.

The difference between loneliness and being alone

Being alone is not a curse. We experience many of the joys in our life when we our alone. For example, reading a book, eating a dessert, listening to good music, etc. These experiences can be enjoyed without having someone else's company.

Love is a demand, not a need. There's nothing wrong with wanting a loving relationship but you must keep in mind that you do not need external love or approval to survive or be happy.

Love and marriage are not necessary and are not enough for happiness. Millions of men and women in the world are married yet unhappy. Love is not an antidote to depression. A lot of times people get depressed even when they love and are loved by their families.

Key Takeaways:

• When you take love as a need, it shows that you need someone else to be worthwhile.

• Being independent does not mean you have to be alone, it means that you can be happy even when you are alone.

• Love and marriage are not necessary and not enough for happiness.

13. Your Work Is Not Your Worth

This chapter looks at the third silent assumption:

"My worth is proportional to my achievements."

The first step to getting rid of this belief is to compare its advantages and disadvantages.

Advantages

• You feel good when you achieve something.

• The belief that your worth comes from your achievements may motivate you to work hard and put extra effort.

Disadvantages

• Focusing on your career or business only will prevent you from other sources of satisfaction in your life.

• If you fail to achieve something, you will feel worthless.

So how can you acquire self-esteem if your worth is not determined by success, approval, or love? There are four paths to self-esteem:

• You must realize that there's no such thing as human worth.

• Keep in mind that you can neither measure nor change your unit of worth. Hence, there's no use worrying about it.

• The only way you lose your self-esteem is by persecuting yourself with negative thoughts.

Self-esteem means treating yourself like a beloved friend.

Key Takeaways:

• Worth and achievement are two different things.

• Human worth can neither be measured nor changed.

• Self-esteem means treating yourself like a beloved friend.

14. Dare to Be Average: Ways to Overcome Perfectionism

Perfection is one of the world's biggest illusions. People who strive for perfection often end up in misery because perfection doesn't exist. It's that fancy, ornate door which promises riches but delivers disappointment.

Techniques for overcoming perfectionism

• Compare the advantages and disadvantages of perfectionism.

• Pick any activity and try to aim for 60% or 80% instead of 100%. Notice how much you enjoy the task and how productive you become.

• Record the amount of satisfaction you get from different activities. Record how perfectly you perform each activity by rating it from 0-100%. This will give you a relationship between perfection and satisfaction.

• Look around and see how you can improve the things around you.

• Giving up perfectionism means confronting your fear of making mistakes. Conquer your fear by refusing to give into perfectionism.

• Use the *vertical-arrow technique* introduced in Chapter 10 to uncover the origin of your perfectionism and the fear of making mistakes. Your silent assumption could be, *"If I make a mistake, my career will be ruined."*

• Be process-oriented. Focus on the process rather than the outcome when you evaluate things.

• Set time limits on your activities. People who are perfectionists are often the real procrastinators because they want to do things thoroughly.

• Defeat your fear of making mistakes by learning to make mistakes.

Key Takeaways:

• People who strive for perfection often end up being unhappy.

• Giving up perfectionism means facing your fear of making mistakes.

PART V: DEFEATING HOPELESSNESS AND SUICIDE

15. The Ultimate Victory: Choosing to Live

Research reveals that the reason behind your suicidal wish is your sense of hopelessness which comes from your twisted thinking. The person sees himself in a trap and thinks there's no way to escape. The most serious mistake people with suicidal impulses make is that they do not talk about it with their counselor. Talking about your suicidal fantasies or urges with your therapist not only gives you a sense of relief, but also a chance to defuse your suicidal thoughts. Fortunately, suicidal urges can be reduced a great extent through cognitive or drug therapy.

Ask yourself, are you taking your suicidal thoughts seriously? Your death wish could either be active or passive.

A **passive death wish** means that you wish you were dead but you are not taking any steps to bring this about.

An **active death wish** means that you are actively preparing for an actual suicide attempt.

In order to assess your suicidal impulse, look at the following symptoms. If one or more of these symptoms applies to you, it means you are in a high-risk group.

• Having severe depression and hopelessness

• Having a history of suicide attempts

• Having made concrete plans for suicide attempt

• Having no deterrents to prevent you from killing yourself

Key Takeaways:

• Hopelessness is a key factor behind your suicidal impulses.

• Don't be afraid of discussing your suicidal fantasies with your therapist.

• Suicidal urges can be reduced significantly through cognitive or drug therapy.

PART VI: COPING WITH THE STRESSES AND STRAINS OF DAILY LIVING

16. How I Practice What I Preach

The cognitive therapy techniques you have learned in the previous chapters can be used in dealing with all sorts of frustrations in your daily life. Dr. Burns shares three examples of how he practices the cognitive techniques he preaches in his personal life.

Coping with hostility

Cognitive therapy techniques help us cope with angry and demanding individuals who vent out their anger on people who care about them the most. One such case was an angry young man who had previously fired twenty doctors. The patient complained of a back pain which was a result of his emotional tension. He had a habit of pointing out faults in his doctors and criticized them during their psychotherapy sessions. The following method helped Dr. Burns control his own frustration and treat the patient.

• Instead of responding to the criticism, urge the patient to say all the negative things he wants to say

• Find some truth in the criticism and agree with him

• Express the disagreements without arguing

• Highlight the importance of continuing with the therapy despite the disagreements

Coping with ingratitude

Some people have the habit of responding to other people's favors with indifference. One such patient had the habit of responding to every suggestion made by the doctor with anger. In order to avoid getting upset over her ingratitude, Dr. Burns used one of his cognitive techniques. He wrote down all his automatic thoughts on a paper and answered them with rational assumptions. For example, *"It's nice to see people appreciate your efforts, but not everyone can be appreciative."* Moreover, he had been blessed with gratitude from his other patients.

Coping with uncertainty and helplessness

When one of his patients suddenly disappeared leaving a suicide note in her possible eighth suicide attempt, Dr. Burns needed his cognitive techniques to cope with the intense uncertainty. Since the evidence of her death wasn't found, he assumed that the patient was alive and that if found alive he would carry on with the treatment. He also realized that he was not responsible for other people's actions and was under no obligation to make his life miserable over his patient's suicide attempt.

Key Takeaways:

• Cognitive therapy techniques can help us deal with the frustrations of our daily lives.

• It can help us cope with angry, demanding, and ungrateful individuals.

PART VII: THE CHEMISTRY OF MOOD

17. The Search for "Black Bile"

This chapter answers some of the most common questions that people ask about depression. These include:

Is depression genetic? Or is it caused by environmental influences?

The answer is still unknown to scientists. Many of the past studies on this issue were quite flawed, hence no conclusion can be drawn based on their outcomes.

Is depression caused by a chemical imbalance in the brain?

Many studies have tried to identify whether depression has anything to do with our brain chemistry but the answer is still unknown. Two arguments have been presented:

• Physical symptoms of depression (agitation, fatigue, insomnia, loss of appetite, etc.) indicate that organic changes may be the cause of depression.

• Hence, abnormal body chemistry may be the cause behind inherited abnormality.

How does our brain work?

Different parts of our brain perform different functions. A part of our brain called the limbic system is responsible for controlling emotions. However, scientists do not know a lot about how our brain creates positive and negative emotions. In fact, our knowledge of how our brain functions is still small.

What goes wrong in depression?

Scientists have not found out the true cause of depression or any other psychological disorder. Of course, there are a lot of theories but none have been definitively proven. The human brain is so complex that scientists have not been able to explain exactly how the firing of a nerve gets transformed into thoughts and feelings.

Key Takeaways:

• The true cause of depression or any other psychological disorder is still unknown.

• We do not know a lot about how our brain creates positive and negative emotions.

• Our knowledge of how our brain functions is still very limited.

18. The Mind-Body Problem

The best approach to treating depression is a combination of psychotherapy and drug medication. Patients who are biologically oriented feel better with drug medication whereas psychologically oriented patients may be comfortable with psychotherapeutic treatment. Regardless of the type of treatment you receive, there are certain irrational thoughts or negative attitudes which can interfere with your treatment.

Myths concerning drug treatment:

Myth #1: *"Taking the drug will make me feel and act strange."* Drug medication will not make you feel or act strange except in rare cases.

Myth #2: *"Drugs are dangerous."* Antidepressant drugs are safer than depression itself. Drug medication shows adverse reactions only rarely.

Myth #3: *"The side effects of the drug medication will be intolerable."* The side effects are mild and usually disappear if you respond favorably to the drug.

Myth #4: *"I'm bound to use the drugs to commit suicide."* Some drugs may be lethal when taken in overdose or combined with other drugs. This concern should be discussed with the physician who may then suggest you a relatively safer drug.

Myth #5: *"I'll become addicted to the drug."* Antidepressant drugs are not addictive and as they begin to work, you will need smaller doses to maintain the effect.

Myth #6: *"Taking drugs would mean I'm crazy."* Antidepressant drugs are given for mood problems not craziness. Moreover, taking the drug may make you feel more 'normal' than leaving the depression untreated.

Myth #7: *"People will look down on me if I take the drug."* They won't know you are using an antidepressant drug unless you tell them. Even if you tell them, people who care about you will understand that you are taking the medication to treat your mood disorder.

Myth #8: *"It's shameful to take a drug. I should treat the depression on my own."* Patients can recover without drug medication with the help of a structured self-help program. However, psychotherapy does not work for every patient and some people recover faster with the help of drug medication.

Some myths concerning psychotherapy:

Myth #1: *"I feel severely depressed and only a drug can help me."* Whether or not you are taking drug medication, willingness to help yourself is a powerful antidepressant in itself. Therefore, combining drug medication with psychotherapy helps speed recovery.

Myth #2: *"Taking psychotherapy would mean I'm weak."* This fear is relatively common in depressed people. It can also be eliminated through the **double standard technique**. The double standard technique is based on the idea that we judge ourselves more harshly than we judge others. Imagine you just found out that your friend received psychotherapy and the treatment helped her a lot. Would you tell them that they are neurotic and that receiving psychotherapy is shameful? If you won't call them neurotic, you shouldn't call yourself that either.

Myth #3: *"My problems are real; psychotherapy cannot solve them."* Cognitive therapy works well with individuals with real problems e.g. medical, bankruptcy, relationship problems etc. On the other hand, depressed people without obvious problems are difficult to treat with psychotherapy.

Myth #4: *"My problems are hopeless. They cannot be treated with psychotherapy or drug medication."* Hopelessness is a symptom of depression and is based on distorted thinking.

Key Takeaways:

• Combining drug medication with psychotherapy helps speed recovery.

• Antidepressant drugs have mild side-effects and show adverse reactions only rarely.

• The willingness to help yourself is of extreme importance whether you take drug medication or psychotherapeutic treatment.

19. What You Need to Know About Commonly Prescribed Antidepressants

Every practitioner has a different approach to the use of antidepressant drugs. It's important to keep in mind that there's no one "correct" approach to drug treatment. Here's what you need to know about common antidepressant drugs:

• The theory that depression results from a chemical imbalance in our brain is still unproven.

• Psychotherapy is as effective as, and sometimes better than, antidepressants. Antidepressants are sometimes helpful but they are not the only solution to your depression.

• In most cases, patients do well with the type of treatment they are comfortable with. So, if you strongly feel that antidepressants will help you then there's a good chance that you will do well with an antidepressant drug.

• Antidepressants must always be used under medical supervision. Patients must not attempt to administer the drug on their own.

• Studies show that 60-70% patients respond to antidepressants. However, the word "respond" is not the same as "recover." Often the improvement is only partial.

• All antidepressant drugs that are currently prescribed by practitioners are known to be equally effective. However, every drug has different side effects and if you are already taking some other type of medicines, not all antidepressants may be safe for you.

• It is not necessary to use two or more antidepressants at the same time. The two drugs in combination may have greater side effects. Of course, there are exceptions to this but one drug at a time usually works well.

• It requires at least 2-3 weeks before a medication begins to show results.

• Many patients fail to respond to one or more drugs. Instead of giving up, try to be persistent and have faith.

• An antidepressant should be taken for 4-5 weeks on average with the right dose in order to check if it's working.

• If an antidepressant drug helps you, you and your doctor mutually decide whether and how long you should continue to take the medication.

• People with certain kinds of depressions may need to stay on the medication for a long time.

• If your depression comes back again, you are more likely to respond to the same antidepressant drug which helped you recover the first time.

Key Takeaways:

• There's no one "correct" approach to drug treatment.

• Psychotherapy is as effective as, and sometimes better than, antidepressants.

• Antidepressants must always be used under medical supervision.

• Apart from an antidepressant, if you are already taking some other type of medicine, tell your doctor about it.

20. The Complete Consumer's Guide to Antidepressant Drug Therapy

This chapter provides a brief overview of the various types of antidepressants drugs prescribed by doctors. The key thing to keep in mind is that if a drug is expensive it doesn't mean it will perform better. Almost all antidepressants are somewhat effective for a variety of problems including depression.

Tricyclic and Tetracyclic Antidepressants

Tricyclic and tetracyclic antidepressants have slightly different chemical structures. Tricyclic drugs contain three molecular rings whereas tetracyclic drugs contain four molecular rings.

The most widely prescribed tricyclic drugs include *Elavil*, *Anafranil*, *Norpramin*, *Sinequan*, *Tofranil*, *Aventyl*, *Vivactil*, and *Surmontil*. These drugs are the least expensive and most effective antidepressants. However, new antidepressant drugs have fewer side effects than tricyclic drugs. Commonly prescribed tetracyclic medications include *Asendin* and *Lu-diomil*. Their side effects are similar to that of tricyclic drugs.

Selective Serotonin Reuptake Inhibitors (SSRIs)

SSRIs are the most popular antidepressant medications at this time. Five commonly prescribed SSRIs include *Celexa*, *Prozac*, *Luvox*, *Paxil*, and *Zoloft*. The side effects of these drugs are more selective than old tricyclic and tetracyclic antidepressants.

Monoamine Oxidase Inhibitors (MAOIs)

MAOIs include *Marplan*, *Nardil*, *Eldepryl*, and *Parnate*. These drugs can be dangerous when combined with some foods and other medications. However, MAOIs can be effective for people who do not respond to other drug medications. Due to this reason, the use of MAOIs has increased in recent years.

Serotonin Antagonists

Serotonin antagonists include *Desyrel* and *Serzone*. They act differently than other antidepressants. These are antianxiety drugs and are especially helpful for people who tend to be worried and nervous.

Bupropion (Wellbutrin)

Bupropion should not be prescribed to people with a history of head injury, brain tumor, epilepsy, bulimia, or anorexia nervosa. It works more like the tricyclic drug *Norpramin*.

Venlafaxine (Effexor)

A relatively new type of drug, *Venlafaxine* is also called a "dual uptake inhibitor." It increases levels of *serotonin* and *norepinephrine*, two chemical messengers in our brain. The same function is also performed by tricyclic drug *Elavil*. *Venlafaxine*, however, is known for having fewer side effects compared to *Elavil*.

Mirtazapine (Remeron)

Just like *Venlafaxine*, *Mirtazapine* increases activity of *serotonin* and *norepinephrine*, but through a different mechanism. *Mirtazapine* has some adverse effects not caused by other drugs.

Mood Stabilizer

Lithium—helpful in situations including acute mania, depression and schizophrenia.

Valproic Acid—used in treatment of bipolar disorder, acute mania, and epilepsy.

Carbamazepine—used in treatment of certain type of epilepsy but also found helpful for manic-depressive patients who do not do well with *lithium*.

Key Takeaways:

• An expensive drug may not necessarily perform better than a cheap one.

• Nearly all antidepressant drugs are somewhat effective for problems other than depression.

39498150R00027

Made in the USA
Middletown, DE
17 January 2017